Published by Furniture Press Books
furniturepressbooks.com

ISBN: 978-1-940092-01-0

Design and layout by Christophe Casamassima

Cover image: *Pieces 3* by Mariah Boyle

ANNOTATED GLASS

ANNOTATED GLASS

Alyse Knorr

[signature]

Ellen —
with all best wishes for
your _literary_ fiction —
Say it loud +
Proud!!

4/11/14

— Alyse

A Furniture Press Book

ACKNOWLEDGMENTS

Grateful acknowledgment is given to the editors of the following publications in which some of these poems, or earlier versions of these poems, first appeared: *Adanna, Birdfeast Magazine, Blood Lotus, BLOOM, Boog City, burntdistrict, Cold Mountain Review, Conclave: A Journal of Character, Counterexample Poetics, CRATE, COYDUP Zine, Elective Affinities, The Fiddleback, Flycatcher, Gargoyle, The Jet Fuel Review, Kestrel, Loose Change Magazine, Lumina, The Nassau Review, New Delta Review, OVS Magazine, Paper Darts, Parcel, The Portland Review, Puerto Del Sol, Redactions, ROAR Magazine, Rock & Sling, Rougarou, Sentence, The Southern Poetry Anthology, The Stillwater Review, Stone Highway Review, Sugar Mule,* and *Used Furniture Review.*

Many thanks to the friends and mentors who supported me in the writing of these poems: Jennifer Atkinson, Jen Daniels, Rachael Graham, Sally Keith, Aubrey Lenahan, M. Mack, Sarah Marcus, Siwar Masannat, Bill Miller, Kara Oakleaf, Eric Pankey, Kate Partridge, Meg Ronan, Katherine Swett, Susan Tichy, Michael Verschelden, Michael Joseph Walsh, Peggy Yocom, and my colleagues at George Mason University. I am grateful to Christophe Casamassima and Furniture Press, and to Mariah Boyle, for their work on this book.

I want to tell about fire.

Gertrude Stein

ANNOTATED GLASS

ALICE IN PUBLIC RESTROOMLAND

In the grimy mirror, her eyes look
even more tunneled than usual.
You'd have to dig pretty deep
to find anything worth excavating
out there, she thinks. By *out there*,
she means, of course, *everywhere*.
And by *everywhere*, she means
in all three stalls and also in the sink-lobby.
What does it mean to add the word
"adventure" to phrases about daily life?
Will my hair catch fire if I light
a match and put my hair in the flame?
Something about mermaids and wet swans.
Even the tiles on the floor have names.

ALICE AT HOME

Made a calendar out of her hair
on the pillow
                    each day marks one
strand less startling there   dark S
swerve in the milk sheets
margin trophy survey of loss

That first night she reached
for my hips dizzy with whiskey
growling between us
                            two women
at the threshold of something
nickel-edged and toxic
                            at the threshold
of her door she put something in
my hand and when I looked
at the bus stop it was change

ALICE AT WORK

Honey locust now ivy now char
looks like fern looks real—must be
the seventh-graders again, one tore up
the rules: scraps of paper lettering the Bible
school halls but from the bottom
up distortion details

Jenny your eyes look like eyes
inside of other eyes the rings
rotate around your arms and one
leg this must be a raindance
only all that falls from the sky is
hello
       you say you want to be
a mountain postcard your hips
closest to the sun back arched
thunderstruck spill but the day
that we met you were moving
and the laws say this will not change

unless
during the lunchtime assembly
someone were to act upon your body
and turn you to wine or glass
or rain

ALICE SLEEP-CLIMBS TO THE SHED ROOF

She doesn't know how she managed the rain-slicked ledges
again, or the loose, rusty gutter. The crickets continue
even this far into October, and Alice takes comfort
knowing it must still be far from morning—far from
the sounds of the trucks rattling down Dickerson
and the buses hissing from stop to stop. The day seeps out
around her, below her, sunlight touching the grass
like a network of nerves speaking each to each.

ALICE DESPAIRS

Long into the night Alice watches
the moon-snaked river before
finally speaking:

So she has left me. Now let bloom here only
small iridescent droplets of speech—
the stories I want to hear told, images
rinsed away from stream to harbor to sea:
let the pines cover one another as they fall
and cicadas hiss among landmines of seed.

ALICE IN BROTHERLAND

When I was young I thought my brother's name was "Own."

His whole life, Owen hated the water. And this was before Rose drowned. Our mother spent her whole life thinking she'd bred this fear by forcing him to swim lessons at the Y, but Owen denied this. He'd just mutter something about wet hair and that'd be it. But no matter how he came by it, you'd see him on every vacation at the beach pacing the shore, scrawny and narrow-eyed behind his hair, shoulders hunched like a witch mid-vision.

ALICE WRITES DOWN EVERYTHING SHE NEEDS TO REMEMBER ABOUT JENNY

to lose weight for a play one month ate only saltine crackers

kept a white bishop in the pocket of her jacket for luck

played Maria

played Juliet

played Christine

played chess

took off all her clothes and led me to a pool on a skyscraper

shoots skeet with a shotgun

smells like an orchestra tuning and the sea

told me a fact about icebergs I didn't know

lives in an old Methodist church

grandmother was a florist

doesn't eat salmon

left side of the bed

blue

ALICE SKETCHES

a man on TV
arms wide mouth cranked
talking to America while a woman
in a column of water dreams
of earth-axis groundcover
and a horizon guaranteed. Staples
dot the walls around the window a
model car spews real pollutants this
is bell-jar living—put me in the
cabinet see it shudder with
my tapping

ALICE IN FATHERLAND

After Rose drowned, our father took up bowling, not drinking. Our mother didn't care about all the nights he spent away in alleys. She'd read about the health benefits of bowling in *AARP Magazine*: the calories burned, tendons and ligaments stretched— not to mention the psychosocial benefits. He was a cranker with a mean hook ball, took me and Owen out for ice cream after his first perfect game. Etc.

ALICE RECALLS GEORGIA TO JENNY

Let me show you the forests submerged in kudzu waist-deep,
the red clay of the riverbed that would stain our hands and fingertips,
or Dock J of the Bald Ridge Marina, where I first fell in love
with a woman when I saw her weeping.

Inside the old revival shacks, grass grows through the boards year-round.
I pass them and remember the story from grade school: a summer night,
june bugs fatter that year than ever, and two girls crashed their pickup
on Campground Road and died.

Give me your hand; I will lick away the orange in the paths of your palms
and we can find a road where I might still be waiting,
among the green growing higher and higher.

ALICE IN LOVE

My eyes knot together
a map from the kit of stars glued
onto the ceiling above her bed
and Jenny spread on top of me
limb against limb, her hot breath
soothing a liturgy into my ear.
Winter boots gauzed in stiff snow
in the corner and it was her feet all along—
that steady footing through silk hillocks
along rows of pines cascading daily, ever-green
ever whispering ever medicated—ever gone
skinny dipping holding some drunk
girl's hand, smelling bourbon on her lips?
It was a concrete gully in the roof,
views of the city on all sides red and yellow
and blinking, the water chlorinated cold, and
how safe I felt today in the valley with Jenny:
her raw, chapped hand pulling me along the
ice-slicked paths. Snow dropping from the pines
in thick rushes. My tongue running the grooves
between your knuckles Jenny your thighs
under the stained glass

ALICE AND JENNY IN THEIR LAND

In the thick-fingered January nights Alice and Jenny build
rooms of oceans and tall ships with oars miles long.
The intricate masts: firm birch braided with cedar,
resin-sealed and sewn with roots thicker than Jenny's wrists.
Moonlight reflects white off the walls of the room and over
the sea. They walk the lengths of the oars, chewing mint leaves
Alice likes to taste on Jenny's fingers and teeth. No sun to rise.
Soft waves grazing the ships. And when Alice builds a spar
high enough to skim the moon, Jenny touches her arm,
watches her lips, and says, *enough*.

ALICE RECALLS HER FIRST MEETING WITH JENNY

I order her fried chicken fingers
and another drink, and there's
her hand on my knee.

My heart crunches into and back
out of its small foil ball, muttering
the same distinct phrase over and over:
This is happening, happening, happening.

ALICE BEGINS

I could say poplar tree
I could say blue
I could say sparrow on a telephone wire
say tender-shingled roof
say citrus smell on my pillow
say snow
I could say wind chimes, two notes
I could say water
say warm bread
say skin

ALICE'S CHILDHOOD

The first thing Owen and I noticed about Rose being dead was that there weren't enough people to play our games anymore. We had created set-ups dependent on the number three, always a hero-villain-damsel system. Without Rose, there was no one to save anymore—the stakes didn't feel as high. I could break out of or into Owen's prisons, duck and storm with my pine branch sword, swim through sharks and squid and lasers and hurricanes, but there was no more hostage, no prisoner to save—no more woman screaming *Please help, my baby, my baby*.

ALICE WALKS WITH JENNY

Grace of your arm hair bent
back in the lake breeze.
Six o'clock sun creeps low, makes
golden shadows on the wake.
This is a place of reaching,
of towns drowned to give us this basin.
Water dropped now to the roofs
of flooded houses and top row of the raceway
grandstands: concrete cresting the sand.
My hands weep for your flesh—
shingles petrified in red clay.

ALICE SPEAKS TO JENNY

I am inside an optical illusion:
when you tie your hair back like that you elude me.

You used to sleep with your fists curled
near your face like a boxer.

Yesterday men in camo scaled up and down my building—
This campaign always works, I heard one of them saying.

I was drunk the night the power went out,
wanting to touch you. Now night and day I drive

the evergreen highway remembering
what you told me about my hands.

Some of the men spoke into walkie-talkies and others held
their palms out flat over their eyes, looking skyward.

And for my hand to move up your dress—
your skin tasting of lavender and cigarettes,

while the trees make shadow fingers across the window glass.
When you tell me I should really take advantage

of this time in my life,
I am watching your mouth

move and trying to prove this
happened—

your crooked fingers
along my hips

ALICE AND JENNY AT THE EDGE

Jenny removes one Camel from the pack at a time.
They've been out on this porch for hours
wrapping words around each other like a glove,
watching the tailights of cars that stir up
puddles of rain with a soft whisper noise.
Alice tries to remember every detail of the night.
She knows she can't bring Jenny back to
the moment with Alice's tongue on each notch of her spine,
knows that now her love is the lizard leaving its tail
behind—an unkempt argument riding her tongue
trying to convince Jenny to return, grant her a pardon
that will re-make everything into the image of two
wax goddesses crouched in a full embrace.

ALICE RECALLS HER FIRST MEETING WITH JENNY

On my way out of her house
that morning I took
a small gourd from a basket
on the kitchen table
and put it in my coat pocket.

All day ran my fingers over
its lumps and ridges, smooth
skin and orange-sheened knots
tucked in my pocket like
a brand-new formula,
the key to a detailed, pulsing map.

AFTER JENNY ASKS ALICE ABOUT HER DEAD SISTER

Shopping, let's go,
there are shrimp on sticks
at Delagio's and lipsticks
of every color and on the way,
there will be yellow tractors mowing
fields of sunflowers whose faces
have turned black.

ALICE IN FATHERLAND

Every other weekend when he came home, Owen and I built him offerings of cardboard and construction paper. Pilfered mother's closet for empty shoeboxes and tiny plastic packets of spare buttons. Dug through the trash for egg cartons and TP rolls. We made aircraft carriers for Owen's tiny die-cast planes and stationed them around the house near our father's shoes, his coffee mug, door to the garage. With each Christmas and birthday, our fleet expanded.

ALICE SKETCHES

a nocturnal ripple stretched flat
across a night desert sand yellow
by day now blue and somehow
evil   a tent pitched in the midst
glows like a candle in a
manhole   perhaps a woman inside
preparing a spell or a torture
ritual   perhaps a mouthful of
pebbles just past her lips
perhaps a bandaged scalp

ALICE SHOVELS SNOW OFF JENNY'S FRONT STEPS

The house spires up above the branches

She cradles the thick wood handle and tells
herself stories from the stained glass, thinks
Didn't Lilith love women

The snow is so white it looks synthetic

She pauses at the tones of a fiddle, looks inside
at Jenny smiling behind red glass, dancing
to a TV commercial   she swirls her hips in fast
steps all alone in the room and Alice shivers

ALICE WALKS WITH JENNY

Beneath this snow and snow and ice, clay. Dirt.
Glass under us and a glass sun above, glass hanging
from trees dripping frozen water yet your steam rises
over us and into the frost-scarred sky. Rough-legged
hawk hunts, hovers above and she whispers *we made it fly*.
My face blurs the surface of the ice. We will break
the water and drink. To sink naked into the frost and lie
here between the two ranges, this nest of cold air. To sleep,
to impose black over all this white—but here we are
touching hands along the ice and we are frozen but do not freeze.

ALICE IN ADOLESCENTLAND

In eighth-grade algebra, Alice knit together equations for amount of blood spilled during an average episode of *Oz* and wrote teen manifestos on her graphing calculator. Then it was architecture she loved, and sketches of levitating mosque-casinos bloomed on the backs of her tests and homework. The teachers were obviously concerned when they saw the grand domes and gold-plated peaks towering among clouds. *Has she fully processed her sister's death? Is this her conception of heaven?* An opulent Vegas palace, a house of worship where cards, money, algebra tests, and sacred text are all just thin scraps from the same pile of wood chips.

JENNY'S HOUSE ELECTROCUTES ALICE

Slick-timbered floor I laid my face on to watch her
feet under the door, and this morning, woke
on her couch to red light filtering down
through the stained glass and ate a peach
on the empty place where the pulpit once stood.

Now, all through the house smell of her
hair wet and floral from the shower—
bad wiring in the walls and she warned me
but here I am on my back
current on my tongue like the inside
of a star and Jenny's terrified face over mine
leaning in

ALICE IN GEORGIALAND

I named the mare O'Malley, saw her every day
on my drive to work, standing still as a pre-blitz pool
in her pasture at the corner of Post and Dickerson.
As a kid once I made a Pegasus—cut a toy knight off
his steed and glued wings in his place. Rose took
it off my desk and carried the thing around with her
for months after, lisping those S's and galloping
the figure across our ice-laced windows and porch.
When my mother found it she shouted at me, said
I'd destroyed something perfectly new.

ALICE ARRIVES AT THE THEATRE

So Alice joins the line-up 30 minutes early

Dropped Jenny off for hair and make-up
two hours ago and spent the rest of the time
husking words out at the mirror seeking
a sweet carol to sing her

Now she scrubs a fleck of marinara
on her shirt collar
considering club soda and the black laces
on the costume bodice Jenny will wear

Here in this diamond-ceiling lobby
Alice makes a decision

to take out her pocketknife
and rip off the stain

IN THEIR LAND

The gaps in the ocean
they cover with islands
and the gaps in the islands
they cover with sieves.

This leads to a permanent
kind of friction
which pleases them—

they who never expected
to find such play here.

When their smoke goes up
over the ships,
they speak gibberish
incantations to provoke
the gods they have made
and the gods they did not make.

They have planned
which fossils to leave
behind but have not
considered when.

They have not considered
the size of the urn
required to hold them.

Each night
with Jenny coiled beside her,
Alice makes small movements
in order to feel and hear
the way Jenny dreams.

And when they wake
and Alice asks her,
Jenny says *like this*

ALICE AND JENNY ARE ESCORTED OFF THE
SOUTHWEST AIRLINES PLANE

The flight attendant says this is a family airline.
This is a family affairline   this is a family lair
I'm saying his is a fantasy error   rewind—this the
famine rare rhyme, the femme-hair kind; firmly blared
sign   forgotten leaking sewer brine.

Boarding pre-air their fingers entwined   hand on
Jenny's knee   the bare shine   kiss
declared un-benign   glare to decide
a plan to wait and see   then snare them, pull aside
two women began a plea   then resigned   this is a despair
guide   an aware collide   the damned pair, blind,   but
still they cut down the trees and prepared their lewd shrine.

So this is a family affair—line   up to see it this is a family
affair this is a family   this is

30

ALICE IN THE FIRST ACT

Jenny, one leg bent up
out of your white dress

The stage floor like an ocean
surface and the lights

diamond-shaped manta rays
winging around you to feed

Your face hidden now
by a crumpled umbrella—

ballet pose or lotus of opening—
To crook my neck around your

arms, into your arms, Jenny,
your eyes not showing

But to move the letters
of your lips into a yes

I could wrap around me
And to float with you over

the smooth-stoned dead sea—

ALICE RECALLS THE BLIZZARD OF '93

Ice on the scarecrow outside and her father's bowling medal clinks against the fridge anytime it's opened. The three kids crowd around the television and watch men beat each other with pipes. Their mother comes downstairs in a sandy-colored skirt with an aspirin in the palm of her hand. She carries it like an offering. Her hand's a mile long and varnished with cracks like the thermometer outside and the telephone sings in waves as the first man runs far away from the second, for good.

ALICE AT THE INTERMISSION

Jenny, more than the scenes with you on stage
in the yellow light, I like the ones without you:
two minor characters expositioning your next
appearance and you off-stage changing from
the short red dress into the hobo costume,
stubbled chin and all, laughing with the stage
manager while you unpeel hose from your little legs.
One minute till you're back on, you reapply
the glue to your fake eyelashes, then return
to a tinkling of applause as I break your fourth wall,
and the next, and the next.

ALICE SKETCHES

a space an emptiness a woman
a potentiality a field a saucer
a man growing older eating chili
out of a paper cup a hole a thought
before it has faded a drain a dress
milk a staff on a page of music
a room a girl shouting an owl
and its eyes a parking lot full a
phone ringing a man on TV who
talks of reading books a moon

ALICE IN GEORGIALAND

They played capture the flag in a bog a mile south of their house. Every Sunday rounded up a few neighbor kids and shorn-hair farmboys and made the hike to their battlefield. One flag a moldy red rug from someone's bathroom. The other a torn blue cape from an old Superman costume. Slough so deep in some places, the water would chill their thighs. Rose, too young to run, played full-time captive. Drifted between the prisons of both sides, welcome in each, pants always soaking. At dusk, Owen would carry her home on his back, Alice following behind.

ALICE CONSIDERS THE TIMING

Another optic net dipped into the waters
of Alice's mind: blood-red valley plunges down
to meet her—no, that was the trip to the Grand
Canyon: kingdom laid out below the three of them
to map like the genes they shared. With Jenny
moaning under her, Alice works through the mechanics
of the scene and feels the temptation to learn
something from this, to take something away.
Were the climate in this realm warmer, she could
dive to the bottom of the ocean and pull up
a lesson, coughing and gasping for air.

ALICE IN THE SECOND ACT

an hour to awe her street black hair
light ribbons it: keys on a clarinet
crow-covered wheat field

      when I blink the birds shuffle
      and ascend

in her living room my shaking fingers
sweat dropped onto the prongs
a jolt a rock through to marrow
her mouth hovered shaping my name
tongue to her lips for the L

IN THEIR LAND

A man sells thousands of balloons on the shore
of the sea they have made. Alice buys them all.
Gives Jenny the pink ones and keeps the yellows,
lets the rest go easing up into the sky. Jenny says,
If I were an old building I'd want to be by the ocean.
Alice gives Jenny the yellow balloons.

ALICE IN SISTERLAND

Each day Rose followed Alice to the bus stop—
a stalking jackal trailing behind her—and Owen not
stalking but stooping to pick up rocks:
these are the kinds of rules Alice hated.
Had not yet learned the phrase *brother's keeper*
but still felt startled with each glance behind her
to see Rose's eyes needled on hers, drilling deep,
a kicked-in mirror, and yes they each had
the yellowgreen eyes of a pruned broom shrub
and yes Rose later steered her bike into such a shrub
in their small Georgia neighborhood and yes the blaring
of her cries could be heard from several streets away.

ALICE AT THE CAST PARTY

She wears a long black dress and we sip cocktails while she tells me how they fake alcoholic drinks in plays.

> *It's just juice—apple for whiskey, cranberry for red wine. You know.*

As she looks at me I notice several new lines on her face and feel like an explorer, so I lean in and kiss her left cheek—chastely. She sighs and says, *Alice.*

Later as I lie in bed with her chastely staring at her ceiling one of us says, *Do you remember?*

And that's when she takes my face in her hands, pulls me close and kisses me on the eyebrow over my left eye: *Yes.*

ALICE IN FATHERLAND

He is now to Alice more driftwood than man, and frequently she imagines him this way: a scrap of washed-up wood sitting on the sofa at the motorhome, taking breaks from the television to play rummy and comb his splintered hair. In this way the degeneration becomes charming to her—artsy and sepia-hued, no more heartbroken than a traffic circle.

ALICE IN BROTHERLAND

Drunk Owen calls Alice to talk about hypocercal pectoral fins and the raise he didn't get at the aquarium this week. Alice listens to him for thirty minutes while watching *That 70s Show* and saying things like *Oh* and *Those bastards* and *Really?* depending on which phrase seems most appropriate according to Owen's tone.

She makes a sandwich and continues Ohing between bites, and then after an hour of his talk she walks out onto her back porch and stares into the hot dark, Owen's voice in one ear and summer crickets in the other.

Sometime after Owen starts weeping, Alice takes off across the grass, running barefoot through the trees, leaves slapping her face and branches winging her arms, until the sound of her breath matches her brother's in the phone still pressed close to her ear and all that's left to do is fall down.

ALICE CORRECTS HERSELF ON SEVERAL POINTS

The river smelled very salty.
I shut myself up in segments, like a telescope,
and dove in. Started swimming.

Now tell me, is this New Zealand or Australia?
Do cats eat bats? Do bats eat cats?
Have you ever tried to curtsy while
you're falling off the earth?

ALICE'S EVIDENCE

She draws on your back with a ballpoint pen You lean away but only your face You let her draw on your back with a ballpoint pen There is a mirror and a woman and a set of fingers around a pen There is a system and an audience There is a dog barking outside Not from hunger or cold but from loneliness The geometry on your back is simple and elegant The room is warm and warmly lit The couch is blue There is a dog The dog is barking

ALICE WISES UP

No girl's puppet, no puppet's lips
when this could just as simply be a
gymnastic genocide, cloud-tarped departure,
caravan of blueprints leaving the scene
with me leading the way.

No no, this line of tape is not for me—
no ma'am, I can sight-read where
I'm headed and tell when someone's
white-walling me— no, *this* captain says
she's the pick and all others can please go

ALICE CONSIDERS ARSON

For to conflag this ship would mean
a kind of tender part after all
and a set of words in my own mouth
to chew on and maybe a Jenny too.
Just to light this etc. now and feed
this blah etc. She set me up and didn't
do love any better. Now for methods,
just number each part of the sentence.
You get a nice list and some heat
and now yes! Jenny can come too,
Jenny the one I'm said to have loved
if there is such a girl

ALICE SPEAKS OF LOVE

Inside a mirror,
width of a cell away—
I can touch it with
the tip of one satin thought.

Line up the chessmen in rows
so that when they start to breathe
I can explain, make them all
fall in love, show them how to
run as fast as they can just
to stay in one place

In the universe beside this one we sit on the same
balcony and you smoke the same cigarette but
when you speak to me the words you say are *yes yes*

ALICE PRETENDS TO BE A MUSEUM EXHIBIT

The aftermath of the photo-op was more complex than she originally
intended. Not *surprise* as in: Happy birthday we're all here
wearing fun hats in your living room, but *surprise* as in: I'm real, look,
I have cells and I am soft to the touch. She feels a compulsory need
to stay in the Ice Age. The mangy wax mammoth keeps her warm all night.
A long line of twine keeps her arm raised high over the saber tooth, one
stone suspended over his cold, sealed skull. She can't remember if she
wanted them to catch her breathing or if she wanted them fooled. She
delights in how her smallest shift hooks all their eyes to her, everyone
looking and slowly, carefully cresting the wave of her secret: *I am here.*

ALICE INCINERATES 1.4 BILLION ACRES OF RAINFOREST

Slow-stroking the matchbox with one finger, she feels
the ribbed surface of the edge and thinks: *pinky bomb*.

With one thwick of her hand, she lights thousands of
matches and throws each one into the nest of something living.

ALICE CREATES 100 NEW JENNYS

Jenny #74: Alice, you are the greatest lover I have ever known

Jenny #6: Alice, hold me

Jenny #99: Alice, who can bury this freight, who can

Jenny #20: toss the scraps

Jenny #2: pledge this and this and

Jenny #74: porous fruit bristling with mold

Jennys (*as a chorus*): where to wait is a language of desire

Jenny #5: *[takes her hand and leads her to the silt shore of a river scattersplit by fish]*

ALICE ORBITS THE MOON AND PREPARES THE LUNAR LANDER

It is white, but
not in a creamy way,
more like bone
or the back of an eye
covered in gray, irregular bruises.

I have covered myself
in hair just for this occasion.
My smile hangs in the air behind me
like a flag, and I'm starting to see
the other side now—

ALICE LEARNS TO THROW KNIVES

Much heavier than she imagined them.
Sharp thwack of each blade inserting
itself into the dinged wood of the target
reminds her of many things etc. etc.
She practices the pinch grip and the hammer,
running her fingers along the spine of each
blade, keeping her wrist and the rest
of her absolutely stiff. Etc. She holds
it tight enough to control the release,
follows the movement from hand to body.
Nails the motion to make it stick.

ALICE RECALLS HER FIRST MEETING WITH JENNY

Striped sage in the menswear section
looking at ties—*Ties earn more tips*
she said *They think it's sexy*
and there I was tucking my scattered
odds away, shaky and squidlike
before my offering, my boilpoint—my love.
Starved for a sip of her mouth then but
the real plague was still months to come.
Now with my last kamikaze breath:
I thought you were all eyes, too.

ALICE THROWS KNIVES

Happily happily but Alice doesn't have any;
Where, with all she has seen and the occurring
dreams of Jenny touching her—parts left
out for the sake of the woman now lying
in her bed, legs wrapped around her—
nowhere left to go but the Apple
Juice Saloon and all its whistlers,
whom Alice has now joined. Bell pepper
bodies dangling from the stools. Alice
impaled on a clicking clicking heel.

ALICE DOES NOT WAKE UP AND REALIZE THIS WAS ALL A DREAM

The next morning, I had even more legs.
No wings no eyes no Jenny or Rose—
I felt visibly invisible, like the moon
during the day. A skate gliding
along sand at the bottom
of the sea, drowned stone coin
gasping for value.

ALICE AT JEKYLL ISLAND

She picks through a boneyard of pine and live oak roots
killed by beach sand the tourists kick up. Passes the ruins
of an old house at Clam Creek: pockmarked wall agape
with missing teeth, stained centerpiece to the ancient
dunes, tidal slough of Glory Beach. Sidney suspension
bridge joins the mass to land with one trembling, silver suture.

She pulls loose threads from the hem of a green dress
as a diet soda metastasizes in her bloodstream.
So long, my three-dimensional beauty—
leave your driftwood smoldering.

ALICE SKETCHES

a cartographic note   small memento
of a girl's high ceiling   arched windows
cold of the bell tower   lacquered floors
spill into egg-white new carpet   soft
enough for a face   and under the latched
door two feet step out of one thing
and into something else

LATER (AUGUST)

sky bereaves in its hot dark coat

cars in the lot huff ozone

checkers clatter the floor

one voice above the rest

all this noise, dear—

I can no longer hear you echo

ALICE'S CHILDHOOD

But there was the winter carnival
Rose thought was in honor of her
turning six, and none of them told her
any differently. Giant tiered floats like
white-frosted cakes, gauzy pink butterflies
teetering on stilts, and a ten-foot tree
raining lights down its sides. Rose stared
at the strong chestnut Clydesdales clopping
down Main Street, and the North Forsyth
Raiders in their red and black marching
uniforms, feathers in their caps trembling
with each step. When the nativity rolled past,
the crowd surged forward to see the plastic
savior. And Owen shoved his way to the edge
of the human path and grabbed a chocolate
Santa Claus, handed it to Rose without a word.
And Alice's mother folded a crane out of
a receipt from her purse and tucked it into
Rose's hair. And Alice held Rose up to see
above the crowd and said, *Look at all of this—*
All of this for you.

ALICE IN THE STUDIO

Jenny, the part of me that lives
with you in your church house
has been quieting

The last dream was weeks ago

You spoke to me about my hands
and I was underwater

We sat on the steps of your house
and I counted your fingers and then
counted them again

Black dress two arcs around your thighs
stains on the bricks, maybe bullet holes
yellow chipped paint

A river between your shoulder blades

Now I paint your legs with long yellow
and white strokes

ALICE WALKS ALONG THE CHATTAHOOCHEE

There are miles left. A man floats
lazy on a blue inner-tube past her,
raises his beer bottle and nods.
In the shallow brown pool at her feet,
a tadpole with back legs. She picks up
a small river pebble, orange-flecked
and smooth, and runs her fingers over it,
puts it in her mouth and tastes the dirt
and all of its ridges and creases. Now.
The stone rolls easy off her fingers,
arcs high above her and enters the water
too far away to make a sound.

ALICE RIDES THE GRAVITY TRAIN

Not in the not-thereafter but wholly present:
the feeling in Alice's chest of both plummeting
descent and suspension. She arrives at the center
of the earth and says to Jenny:

"When two people make love for the first
time, each is wondering how it will feel
for the other. When I say forever, I don't
mean tomorrow. I mean the way the smoke
from your mouth rises and disappears
at the same time. The way the trees are black."

Jenny reaches for Alice's hand but Alice's
hand is a bird. The iron around them hums
and tremors, and Alice closes her eyes
to hear these sounds more accurately.
What she will carry back to the surface
is a permanent light swaddled in old leaves.

ALICE BEGINS

She has never worked with marble before.
Soapstone, yes, and alabaster. She roughs out
the stone and cuts in thin grooves against
the contour of the rock. She chisels deeper,
shaping out a nose, eye hollows, pair of lips.
She delights in the first shadows she can see
emerging under the face's nostrils—the light now
playing off this new angle she has created.
Clavicles curve up under the neck, and she chips in
irises, eyebrows. As the weeks and the project
proceed she realizes first that the face is familiar,
and later that it is her own.

HOW WILL I

You will take another bandage
and wrap it around your feet
You will keep walking
You will hold the forest
in your arms and then place it
inside your mouth for one day
You will keep walking
You will name everything you see
because everything you see
has a name you know

ALICE IN ROSELAND

Alice dreams of an enormous house—pale clapboard
hunched among tangles of briar, stripped of an address,
dozens of women living inside. A railroad bisects
the first floor, and the Amtrak trains keep the women
hovering above their sleep all night. Rose enters all
the rooms at once searching for Alice, tracking mud
through the halls of the house in small round clumps.
She grows lost. She sits down to weep her permanent tears.
The women emerge one by one, with Alice at the end
of the line. A steam engine comes to a trembling halt
in the kitchen. Rose tugs at Alice's hand, reaches up
with her late-flowered eyes. Slowly, Alice stoops to press
her lips against Rose's windfall skull. She hums a song
from an old cartoon, counts the verses, then lifts Rose
onto the train.

ALICE PLANTS A TREE

She digs a small, black-dirt hole
and lifts the sapling by its burlap ball,
fingering the tiny string roots, soft and fine,
smaller than veins. The afternoon moon
appears as a pale white thumbprint.
With her bare hands she pats earth around the base,
digs the tips of her fingers into the moist surface.
After she is finished, she stands and considers
the tree, waist-high and not quite yet a tree.
When the spring wind starts up, the tiny leaves
tremble and the stick trunk bows and then straightens.